# A HEART FULL OF TURQUOISE

## Pueblo Indian Tales
## retold by Joe Hayes

Illustrations & Design by Lucy Jelinek

A Mariposa Book

Published by
Mariposa Publishing
922 Baca Street
Santa Fe, New Mexico 87501
(505) 988-5582

FIRST EDITION 1988

Selections from "The Day It Snowed Tortillas," "Coyote &," "The Checker Playing Hound Dog" and "A Heart Full Of Turquoise" by Joe Hayes available on cassette tapes from Trails West Publishing, P.O. Box 8619, Santa Fe, New Mexico 87504-8619.

Also from Trails West Publishing — bilingual picture books:

MARIPOSA, MARIPOSA
The Happy Tale of La Mariposa — The Butterfly

MONDAY, TUESDAY, WEDNESDAY, OH!
LUNES, MARTES, MIERCOLES, O!

THE TERRIBLE TRAGADABAS
EL TERRIBLE TRAGADABAS

NO WAY, JOSÉ!
¡DE NINGUNA MANERA, JOSÉ!

ISBN 0-933553-05-6

To my mother
Marie J. Hayes

# Also by Joe Hayes
## from Mariposa Publishing

**The Day It Snowed Tortillas**
Tales from Spanish New Mexico

**Coyote &**
Native American Folk Tales

**The Checker Playing Hound Dog**
Tall Tales from A
Southwestern Storyteller

# TABLE OF CONTENTS

# INTRODUCTION

This book is a collection of some of my favorite Pueblo tales. I like them because each one has something in it that pleases my imagination or seems just right for my way of story-telling. These aren't necessarily the most common or typical Pueblo tales, just the ones I like best.

I learned these stories from reading other writers' books. Usually the other writers were anthropologists, scientists who study culture, and they collected the stories fifty or more years ago from Indians in the pueblos. From those collections I got the basic idea of the stories, and then made up my own way to tell them. Sometimes I changed a story, adding new characters, or dropping out some incidents. Often I added repetition or refrains because I find that listeners like to say and do things with me when I tell a story.

So these can't really be considered traditional tales, but I have tried to keep the same feeling in each story that I sensed when I first discovered it. I hope readers will take the same delight in these stories that I do, and maybe some will find them so appealing that they will learn them and begin telling them themselves.

# THE SINGING WAGON

BLACK BEETLE OLD MAN and Black Beetle Old Woman lived at the top of a small hill. In the valley below them lived many other animals.

One day Black Beetle Old Woman wanted to bake bread, so she told her husband, "Go and get me some firewood to heat my oven."

Black Beetle Old Man had a wagon with big wooden wheels that he used to haul wood. He went outside and took hold of the handles of the wagon with his two front legs, and with his other legs he walked off pulling the wagon behind him. The empty wagon was light, and Black Beetle Old Man walked fast. The wooden wheels of the wagon rolled along silently.

Black Beetle Old Man walked down the hill and over to the river. He found many dead branches in the thicket near the river and he broke them up for firewood. He filled his wagon and then started back toward his house.

Now that the wagon was full, it moved slowly. And the wooden wheels squeaked as they rolled along —

Aii, aii, aii . . .

Tseeneh, tseeneh, tseeneh . . .

Aii, aii, aii . . .

Tseeneh, tseeneh, tseeneh . . .

It almost sounded like a song!

Black Beetle Old Man walked until he got close to the little hill below his house. Then he thought, "I'll never be able to pull this wagon up the hill all by myself. I'd better go find someone to help me."

Coyote lived nearby, so Black Beetle Old Man walked off to Coyote's house and asked Coyote to help him. Together Black Beetle Old Man and Coyote went to where the wagonload of wood was waiting. Coyote said, "Black Beetle Old Man, you pull the wagon from in front, and I'll push the back of the wagon."

So they started out. And the wagon wheels began to squeak —

Aii, aii, aii . . .

Tseeneh, tseeneh, tseeneh . . .

Coyote said to himself, "What a pretty song this wagon sings. I could dance to that song!"

Black Beetle Old Man huffed and puffed as he pulled the wagon. But instead of pushing the back

of the wagon, Coyote danced along behind lifting his
knees up high and singing —
    Aii, aii, aii . . .
    Tseeneh, tseeneh, tseeneh . . .

When they got to the very bottom of the hill, Coyote called out, "Black Beetle Old Man, wait! Don't pull your wagon up the hill yet. I want my friend Badger to learn the song your wagon sings. Push it back to where it was while I run and bring my friend."

So while Coyote ran to Badger's house, Black Beetle Old Man pushed his wagonload of firewood back to where he had left it when he went to get Coyote's help. Just about the time he got to the spot, Coyote arrived with his friend.

Black Beetle Old Man took hold of the handles of the wagon and started out again while Coyote and Badger pushed from behind. Soon the wheels began to squeak —

Aii, aii, aii . . .

Tseeneh, tseeneh, tseeneh . . .

Black Beetle Old Man huffed and puffed and sweated as he pulled the wagon. Coyote danced along lifting his knees up high. And Badger bobbed his head from one side to the other and sang —

Aii, aii, aii . . .

Tseeneh, tseeneh, tseeneh . . .

When they reached the bottom of the hill, Badger said, "Black Beetle Old Man, wait! Don't pull your wagon up the hill yet. I want my friend Skunk to learn the song your wagon sings."

Black Beetle Old Man pushed his wagon away from the hill again while Badger padded off to Skunk's house.

Black Beetle Old Man took the handles of the wagon again and started out. Coyote and Badger and

Skunk gave a shove from behind. And the wheels squeaked —

Aii, aii, aii . . .

Tseeneh, tseeneh, tseeneh . . .

Black Beetle Old Man huffed and puffed and sweated and strained as he pulled the wagon. Coyote lifted his knees high as he danced. Badger bobbed his head from side to side. And Skunk waved his tail up and down.

Everyone knows what happens when Skunk starts to wave his tail around! Coyote was the first one to stop singing. He fanned a paw in front of his nose. "Whew!" he said. "I think I'd better leave. My wife will be wondering where I am." And Coyote ran away.

Then Badger turned his long nose away from Skunk and said, "I'd better go too. I was in the middle of digging a new hole when Coyote came to get me. I'd better go and finish the job." And Badger ran away.

But Skunk knew the real reason why they were leaving, and he was embarrassed. Skunk went away too.

Black Beetle Old Man had to pull the wagon up the hill all by himself. When he got home, Black Beetle Old Man was finally able to sing the song himself. While he unloaded the wagon, he sang —

Aii, aii, aii . . .

Tseeneh, tseeneh, tseeneh . . .

Black Beetle Old Woman came outside and said, "Oh! That's a beautiful song you're singing. I wish we had a baby to sing it to."

So Black Beetle Old Man and Black Beetle Old Woman made a little doll out of rags and all evening long they sat and sang to it —

Aii, aii, aii . . .

Tseeneh, tseeneh, tseeneh . . .

Finally they both fell asleep. When they woke up the next morning they couldn't remember the song. Since the wagon was empty now, it was no longer singing. And the song was forgotten.

But someone must have remembered the song because they still tell this story about it!

# BE CAREFUL
# WITH PROMISES

ONE SUMMER YELLOW CORN GIRL worked very hard on her garden. She dug up the soil very deep and raked it over and over again until every lump was broken. Then she planted corn and beans and melons and squash. When the green plants began to grow, she watered them faithfully and pulled up every weed that showed itself above the ground. If a bug took a single bite out of a leaf in her garden, Yellow Corn Girl hunted all over until she found that bug and squashed it. Yellow Corn Girl's garden was the prettiest one in the pueblo, and she was very proud of it.

One morning as Yellow Corn Girl was on her way to visit her garden she heard someone singing from a clump of grass nearby —

Hai-lai-lai-lai, hai-lai-lai-lai . . .
Corn, beans, melons, and squash,
Good to eat, good to eat.

The song sounded so pretty to Yellow Corn Girl that she walked over closer to see who was singing. But when she got close to the clump of grass, the song stopped.

Yellow Corn Girl shrugged and walked away. But when she was just a short distance from the clump of grass, the song began again —

Hai-lai-lai-lai, hai-lai-lai-lai . . .
Corn, beans, melons, and squash,
Good to eat, good to eat.

Yellow Corn Girl turned and walked back toward the grass. But the song stopped. She walked away, and the song began again. The same thing happened the third time she came near the grass.

And then, the fourth time Yellow Corn Girl approached the clump of grass, she saw who was singing. It was Grasshopper. "Grasshopper," said Yellow Corn Girl, "please don't stop singing when I come close to

you. I want to learn your song. It's so pretty, and I can sing it to myself when I'm working in my garden."

But Grasshopper said to Yellow Corn Girl, "No. I won't sing for you. If I tried to go into your garden, you would chase me away. You'd even hit me with a rock if you could. You won't share your garden with me, so why should I share my song with you?"

"But, Grasshopper," Yellow Corn Girl explained, "my mother and father will be angry with me if I let anything happen to my garden. Please sing for me just one more time."

"If I sing for you one time, will you let me go into your garden just once?"

Yellow Corn Girl really wanted to learn that pretty song. She said, "Yes, if you sing for me I will let you go into my garden one time."

"But, Yellow Corn Girl," Grasshopper said, "what about the rest of my family? They need food too. It won't be any fun for me to eat if I know my brothers and sisters are going hungry."

"They may go into the garden too," said Yellow Corn Girl. "But just once. Now, teach me your song!"

Grasshopper sang for Yellow Corn Girl until she learned the song. She went away singing —

Hai-lai-lai-lai, hai-lai-lai-lai . . .

Corn, beans, melons, and squash,

Good to eat, good to eat.

Yellow Corn Girl sang the song to herself all afternoon as she worked in her garden, and all evening as she ground corn in her house.

The next day Yellow Corn Girl went to visit her garden and as she approached it she heard many, many voices singing —

HAI-LAI-LAI-LAI, HAI-LAI-LAI-LAI . . .
CORN, BEANS, MELONS, AND SQUASH,
GOOD TO EAT, GOOD TO EAT.

She hurried to find out who the voices belonged to.

She found her garden full of grasshoppers! They had eaten all the leaves off the bean plants and the blossoms off the squash. The corn had been stripped down to bare stalks. At the edge of the garden she saw Grasshopper. "You have ruined my garden!" sobbed Yellow Corn Girl.

But Grasshopper just smiled and said, "You told me I could invite my brothers and sisters to eat in your garden. That is all I have done."

And the grasshoppers ate and ate until there wasn't a bite left in the garden. Then they flew away singing —

Hai-lai-lai-lai, hai-lai-lai-lai . . .
Corn, beans, melons, and squash,
Good to eat, good to eat.

Poor Yellow Corn Girl had nothing left to show for all her work but a song, and she was too unhappy to sing it. She and her family were very hungry that year.

And when old ones tell the children this story they add, "See what can happen when you make a promise? Don't be like Yellow Corn Girl. Be careful what promises you make!"

# CLAY OLD MAN
# AND CLAY
# OLD WOMAN

IN THE BEGINNING THE PEOPLE didn't know how to work with clay. They had no pots to cook their food in. They had to roast it over an open fire. And they had to eat out of their own hands, because they had no bowls. They had to carry water from the springs and rivers in a hollow gourd.

But in the land below, Thought Woman, the Mother of All, knew of the people's need for better vessels, and she thought of pottery. From clay she made a man and a woman. She said to the woman, "You will be Clay Old Woman." She said to the man, "You will be Clay Old Man." Then she told them to go teach the people about pottery.

Clay Old Woman and Clay Old Man came up out of the land below and into this world and they started toward the pueblo. They were dressed all in white, and their faces were white with red eyes. Clay Old Man walked with a stick and carried a basket full of clay on his back. When the people saw them coming, they wondered who they were and why they had come.

Clay Old Woman and Clay Old Man came into the pueblo and went straight to the dance plaza. Clay Old Woman took the clay from Clay Old Man's basket. She sat down and began to mix sand with it and moisten it with water. Clay Old Man danced around her as she worked.

When the clay was ready, Clay Old Woman began to make a pot. Clay Old Man danced faster.

Clay Old Woman worked a long time, making a pot that stood nearly as high as her head as she sat there on the ground. The bigger Clay Old Woman

made the pot, the more wildly Clay Old Man danced. Then, when the pot was almost finished, Clay Old Man bumped into it. It fell over and broke into pieces.

Clay Old Woman was angry! She grabbed Clay Old Man's stick and chased him around the plaza. Finally she caught Clay Old Man and began to scold him. For a long time they argued. Then they made up, and walked back to the broken pot together.

Clay Old Man gathered the pieces of the broken pot together and rolled them into a ball again. Then he walked all around the plaza, giving a piece of the clay to each woman in the pueblo. They all sat down and began to make a pot, just as they had seen Clay Old Woman do.

Clay Old Man told the women, "Now you know how to work with clay. You can make many useful things with it. This is something that has been sent to you by the Mother of All. Don't ever stop making pottery."

From that day on the people began to work with clay. They made cooking pots and bowls and big, round storage jars. They made water jars to carry water home from the springs. They made pottery that was very useful and pottery that was beautiful to look at.

Today, the Pueblo Indians still work with clay. They make some of the finest, most beautiful pottery in the world. They say they will always make pottery because it is a gift that was sent to them by the Mother of All, and as Clay Old Man told them, they must never stop using that gift.

# FROG
# AND
# LOCUST

ONCE IT DIDN'T RAIN for a whole year. The grass turned brown and died. Trees and bushes lost their leaves. In the canyon bottom, where a lively stream usually flowed, there were just a few puddles of water left. And every day those puddles got smaller and smaller.

Living at the edge of one puddle was a frog. The frog saw his puddle get smaller with each passing day, and he knew that if it didn't rain the puddle would soon dry up. And he would die!

But the frog knew how to sing a rain song. So he sang to see if he could bring some rain. The frog croaked —

R-R-RAIN, R-R-RAIN, R-R-RAIN . . .

But his song wasn't loud enough to reach the top of the mountain, and that is where the Rain God lived. The Rain God couldn't hear the frog singing, and no rain came.

Not far from the frog's puddle was a bush, and living in the bush was a locust. The locust knew that if it didn't rain, he wouldn't live through the summer. So as he clung to the bush the locust buzzed —

R-r-r-rain-n-n-n, r-r-r-rain-n-n-n . . .

But that song wasn't loud enough to reach the top of the mountain either. And when the locust saw that there were no clouds in the sky, and it wasn't going to rain, he started to cry —

Ee-he-he-he-he . . .

The frog heard someone crying, so he hopped over there. He looked up and croaked —

WHAT'S THE MATTER-R-R . .?

WHAT'S THE MATTER-R-R . .?

The locust told him, "If it doesn't rain, I'm going to die!"

When the frog heard that, he thought about how the same thing would happen to him if it didn't rain, and he started to cry too —

WAH-WAH-WAH . . .

But then the locust got an idea. He thought — when one person works all alone, he doesn't get much done. But when people work together, they can do a lot of work. So the locust said, "Frog, maybe we should sing together."

The frog thought that was a good idea. So they added their songs together —

R-R-RAIN ... r-r-r-rain-n-n ...
R-R-RAIN ... r-r-r-rain-n-n ...

It still wasn't loud enough to go to the top of the
mountain. But it was loud enough to go to the next puddle up the canyon. And living over there was another
frog. On the other side of the canyon, there were even
more frogs. They heard the frog sing and thought they
would join in and sing along with him. They all sang —

R-R-RAIN, R-R-RAIN, R-R-RAIN ...

In nearby bushes, and in the bunches of grass
still growing at the puddle's edge, there were also more
locusts. They heard the song and thought they'd join
in too —

R-r-r-rain-n-n, r-r-rain-n-n ...

Soon all the frogs and locusts were singing —

R-R-RAIN ... r-r-r-rain-n-n ...
R-R-RAIN ... r-r-r-rain-n-n ...

It was a loud song! It went clear to the top of
the mountain!

The Rain God heard the song. He climbed up to the center of the sky and gathered dark clouds all around him. From the distant mountains he made the cool wind begin to blow. Rain drops started falling. The rain fell faster . . . and faster. It was a big storm!

The canyon stream filled back up with water. The trees and bushes got new leaves. The whole land came to life again. And it was all because the frogs and locusts worked together!

And that's why it is to this day that if one person's fields are dry and dying, he doesn't go off by himself and sing for rain. But all the people gather together. They dance with one heart, and with one voice they sing. And in that way they can always bring the rain.

# CLAY POT BOY

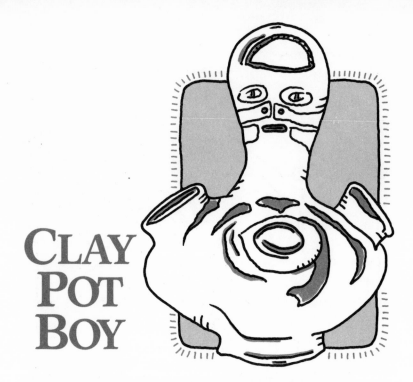

ONCE THERE WAS A PUEBLO GIRL who was not at all interested in boys. When she ground corn, boys would come and stand outside the window and try to talk to her. But she paid no attention. Instead of going to fetch water with groups of girls so that she might stop and talk to boys on the way back from the spring, she went silently to the spring by herself. She never attended the dances or games where boys and girls met.

The girl's old father and mother didn't understand their daughter. They wanted her to get married and have children, as other girls did. But they couldn't complain because their daughter was a good worker and always helped with any chores that needed to be done.

The old woman made water jars, and the girl helped by preparing the clay. She would grind dry clay very fine, and then add water to it. She would work the clay with her bare foot, kneading and rolling it and adding more water until it was just right for her mother to build into a clay pot.

The mother always gathered her clay by the edge of a spring, not far from the pueblo. One day when she went to the spring to get clay, she happened to be thinking about how her daughter didn't care for boys and would probably never marry and have a child. The spirit who lived in the water of the spring heard the old woman's thoughts. He placed a seed of life in the clay she was gathering.

Later that day when the girl was working the clay, the seed of life entered her and a baby began to grow inside her.

In time she had her child, but it wasn't a human baby at all. It was a clay pot! The old woman was very angry. "What will the people say?" she worried. "My daughter has given birth to a clay pot."

But when the old man came home and learned what had happened, he was very happy. "Now I will have a grandson to keep me company," he said, "and to train in the ways of our people. We'll call him Clay Pot Boy."

Clay Pot Boy had no arms or legs, but he had a mouth at the top, and they fed him through this opening. He grew very fast. In just twenty days he could join in the games of boys who were nine or ten years old. Of course he couldn't run, but he could roll along as fast as any of them ran. The boys were happy to include Clay Pot Boy in their fun.

Then one evening in late fall, as the old man sat telling Clay Pot Boy the stories of their people, a light snow began to fall outside. Clay Pot Boy said, "Grandfather, take me rabbit hunting tomorrow. You have told me that the best time to hunt rabbits is the morning after a light snow."

"You can't hunt rabbits," the grandfather told him. "You have no arms to shoot a bow with."

But Clay Pot Boy told him, "I could roll ahead and scare the rabbits from their hiding places. I'll chase them back toward you, and you can shoot them."

So the next morning before sunrise the grand-father and Clay Pot Boy started out to hunt rabbits. They had gone just a short way from the pueblo when they saw rabbit tracks in the fresh snow, and Clay Pot Boy rolled ahead, following the tracks.

Clay Pot Boy followed the rabbit tracks across the valley. Then he rolled up one side of a hill and started down the other. As he rolled down the other side of the hill he began to gather more and more speed. He wasn't able to stop when he reached the bottom and crashed against a big rock. Clay Pot Boy was shattered into pieces.

Up from the broken chips of pottery stood a strong, handsome boy. He looked suprised and touched his chest and arms and legs in amazement. Then he shrugged his shoulders and ran off along the rabbit trail.

He was a fast runner, and soon caught the rab-bit. Then he ran off following another rabbit trail, and caught that one. Before morning was over he caught several more. Then he returned to find his grandfather.

Clay Pot Boy found his grandfather sitting on a rock looking very sad. "Hello, Grandfather," he said. But the old man didn't recognize Clay Pot Boy. He thought he was just a strange boy who had said "grand-father" to be polite to an old man.

"Have you seen a clay pot rolling along?" the grandfather asked. "Have you seen my grandson who looks like a clay pot?"

Clay Pot Boy thought he would tease his grand-father. "No," he answered, "I didn't see anyone or anything except these rabbits." And he held up the bunch of rabbits he had caught.

Grandfather looked even sadder, and Clay Pot Boy felt sorry for him. He couldn't tease his grandfather any more. "Grandfather," he said, "I am your grandson. I am Clay Pot Boy."

At first his grandfather didn't believe him, but when Clay Pot Boy talked of all the things they had done together, Grandfather knew this handsome boy was his grandson. He was very happy.

Clay Pot Boy and his grandfather returned home. They told Clay Pot Boy's mother and grandmother what had happened, and they all began a happy life together.

But one thing caused Clay Pot Boy some sadness. He didn't know who his father was. Often he would ask his mother, and she would tell him, "You don't have a father."

Clay Pot Boy would insist, "But I must have a father." And finally one day he told his mother, "I am going to find my father. I won't come back until I do." And he left the pueblo.

The trail Clay Pot Boy took away from the pueblo led past the spring where his grandmother always gathered her clay, and as he came near to the spring Clay Pot Boy saw a man sitting beside the water. The man asked Clay Pot Boy, "Where are you going?"

"I am going to look for my father."

"Who is your father?"

And Clay Pot Boy answered, "I think you are my father."

"I can't be your father," said the man. And he looked sternly at Clay Pot Boy, trying to frighten him.

But Clay Pot Boy wasn't frightened. "Yes," he said, "I'm sure of it. I'm sure that you are my father."

Then the man smiled. "I am your father," he said. And he told Clay Pot Boy that he lived below the waters of the spring. He took Clay Pot Boy with him into the spring, and they traveled down and down until they reached a land below the water.

Clay Pot Boy saw green trees and grass and flowers all around. The people of that land were friendly. They all came out to greet Clay Pot Boy and welcome him into their world.

Clay Pot Boy traveled all about with his father discovering the wonders of the land below the spring. With each new beauty his father showed him, Clay

Pot Boy would say, "Oh, I wish my mother could see this!" And always when he said that, his father looked a little strange.

After four days, Clay Pot Boy told his father that he wanted to return to his mother's pueblo. His father brought him back up through the waters of the spring and said goodbye.

When Clay Pot Boy arrived home, he found that his mother was very sick. They tried every medicine they knew to cure her. They sang every healing chant and said every prayer, but Clay Pot Boy's mother died.

Then Clay Pot Boy thought, "There's nothing left for me here. I will go back and live with my father's people below the water." He walked back to the spring, and found his father waiting there beside the water. Together they traveled down to the land beneath the spring.

When they arrived below the water, Clay Pot Boy was very surprised to find his mother waiting for him in that land. His father explained that the land below the water was a spirit land, and that the only way Clay Pot Boy's mother could come there was to die in the land above.

So now a truly happy life began for them all. And if you should ever go and sit beside that spring, you will hear the laughter of Clay Pot Boy and his father and mother in that beautiful land below the water.

# A HEART FULL OF TURQUOISE

ONCE THERE WAS AN EVIL GIANT living in
a cave in the mountains not far from a pueblo. One day
just at noon the giant came striding toward the pueblo
with a basket on his back. He chanted as he came —
Think I want to eat some good corn.
Think I want to eat some good corn.
The people of the pueblo heard the giant when
he was still far off and they were frightened. They
thought the giant might knock down their houses if

they didn't feed him. So they gave corn to the giant, until all the corn they had stored in the pueblo was gone. The giant filled his basket with the corn and then went away.

The people said among themselves, "It will be a hard year without the corn we had stored away, but at least the giant didn't destroy our village."

The next day at noon the giant came toward the village chanting —

Think I want to eat some melons.

Think I want to eat some melons.

The people carried melons out to the giant. He filled his basket and then left. It had taken all the melons they had in the pueblo to fill the giant's basket.

On the third day when the giant came treading toward the pueblo, he chanted —

Think I want to eat some deer meat.

Think I want to eat some deer meat.

Hunters from the pueblo had been very successful that year and there was much dried deer meat stored away in the village. But it took the full store of deer meat to fill the giant's basket.

Then the people began asking one another, "What will the giant want next? He has already taken all the food we have in our village."

At noon the next day the giant came striding toward the pueblo again. From far off the people heard him chanting —

Think I want to eat some children.

Think I want to eat some children.

"Listen!" the people said. "He is asking for our children. What can we do?"

Their medicine man told them, "We must pray and ask Our Mother to make us a good giant to fight this evil one."

The medicine man gathered all the people together in the plaza. He brought out a perfect ear of white corn and laid it on the ground. He covered the ear with a large white cloth and then began to sing a holy song and sprinkle corn meal on the cloth.

A shape began to move under the cloth. The shape grew bigger and bigger. Soon a giant sat up and threw the cloth aside. He asked the people, "What have I been made for?"

The medicine man told him, "Our Mother has sent you to help us fight an evil giant who wants to eat our children."

"Oh," said the giant. "Then I will help you." And he stood up and looked all about.

The bad giant was just getting close to the pueblo, still singing —

Think I want to eat some children.
Think I want to eat some children.

The good giant heard the song, and he sang back to the evil giant —

You're not going to eat these children.

You're not going to eat these children.

The evil giant stopped in his tracks. He looked first to the left, and then to the right. Then he sang —

Who thinks he can tell me that?

Who thinks he can tell me that?

The good giant sang —

I'll tell you whatever I want to.

I'll tell you whatever I want to.

Then the evil giant challenged the good giant to a fight. The medicine man made a trail of corn meal and led the good giant out of the village toward where the evil giant was standing. The evil giant had a big war club in his right hand. The good giant had a long knife made of black obsidian in his belt.

The good giant told the evil one, "You are evil, so you must hit first. Hit me four times with your club. Then if I can, I will strike you with my knife."

The first time the evil giant hit the good giant, the club bounced off so fast it almost flew out of the evil giant's hand. The good giant didn't even blink.

The second time the evil giant struck, there was a cracking sound. But it was the wood of the club cracking. The good giant wasn't hurt at all.

With the third blow the club split down the middle. And the fourth blow shattered the evil giant's war club into splinters.

Then the good giant struck with his long stone knife and the evil giant's heart was cut wide open. The men from the pueblo ran up to him and saw that his heart was filled with thorns and cactus needles. The medicine man took the cactus and thorns from the evil giant's heart and filled it with turquoise and pink quartz so that it would no longer be evil. He put the giant back together.

The medicine man made a trail of corn meal leading the good giant back into the pueblo. He covered him with the white cloth and sang him back to an ear of corn. All the people thanked Our Mother for sending the good giant to help them.

Then with another trail of corn meal the medicine man led the other giant back to his cave in the mountains. And since the giant's heart had been made good, he never returned to bother the people of the pueblo.

# THE GIRL
# WHO MARRIED
# THE RAINBOW

LONG AGO THERE WAS A GIRL named White
Corn Girl. She lived with her father and mother, and
like all good Pueblo girls she worked hard to help her
parents. She cooked and ground corn into fine, light
meal. She tended the family garden. And each evening
she went to the spring with her water jar to bring
water for the next day's cooking.

Of course, those were the same chores done by every girl in the pueblo, but White Corn Girl did her work with such a happy, quiet heart that every task seemed to turn out better for her. The corn she ground was always finer than anyone else's. Her garden grew greener, and even the water she carried gracefully from the spring seemed to have a sweeter taste to it.

Everyone in the pueblo talked about what a remarkable girl White Corn Girl was. Even people in neighboring pueblos spoke of her cheerfulness and grace. Finally Rainbow Boy, who lived in the sky, heard of White Corn Girl.

One evening Rainbow Boy went to the spring just before White Corn Girl came with her water jar. He left a beautiful clear crystal on the ground beside the spring and hid in the bushes nearby. When White Corn Girl bent down to fill her jar, she saw the crystal sparkling on the ground and picked it up.

Rainbow Boy came out of his hiding place and asked, "Did you see a crystal here on the ground? I have lost one."

White Corn Girl didn't know what to say. She didn't want Rainbow Boy to think she was trying to steal his crystal. "No," she told him. "Maybe it is over on the other side of the spring."

She hoped he would go over to the other side of the spring to look and give her a chance to drop the crystal back on the ground, but Rainbow Boy smiled and said to her, "You have the crystal in your hand. I can see all the colors reflecting on your face."

White Corn Girl was very embarrassed. But Rainbow Boy told her, "That's all right. You may have the crystal. And I have even finer gifts for you if you will come and visit me in my home."

White Corn Girl agreed to go with him to his home, so they set out walking to the east. They walked and walked, and White Corn Girl began to grow tired. "Your home is very far away," she said to Rainbow Boy.

"Close your eyes and I'll get us there quickly," Rainbow Boy replied. And when White Corn Girl closed her eyes, Rainbow Boy made a many-colored ladder appear. They traveled quickly up the ladder to his home in the sky.

Rainbow Boy's home was filled with light. There were many precious stones inside, and bright colored birds sat on the rungs of the ladders singing beautifully. Everything White Corn Girl admired, Rainbow Boy gave her as a gift. Rainbow Boy's mother treated White Corn Girl kindly, and White Corn Girl ground fine corn meal for her to show what a hard worker she was.

Then White Corn Girl told Rainbow Boy she wanted to return to her own home. Again he told her to close her eyes, and made a rainbow ladder back to earth for them to go down.

Before he left her, Rainbow Boy asked White Corn Girl if she would marry him and come to live in his home in the sky. White Corn Girl said she would, and Rainbow Boy told her he would meet her at the spring in four days to take her away.

But Coyote happened to be lurking in the bushes nearby, and he heard what White Corn Girl and Rainbow Boy said. Coyote had always wanted to win White Corn Girl for his own wife, and now he thought of a good trick to get her.

Coyote knew that on the four evenings White Corn Girl had left at home, she would go to the spring to get water for her parents, just as before. So on the third day after White Corn Girl returned home, Coyote got out his finest clothes and set them on the floor in front of him.

Coyote pulled on his white buckskin moccasins. He stamped his foot four times and then sang to himself, "Do I look handsome? Yes, I look handsome."

He tied skunk fur tufts around his ankles. He stamped his foot again and sang, "Do I look handsome? Yes, I look handsome."

He put on his leggings, and his white woven shirt and colored sash. He tied shell beads around his neck and parrot feathers in his hair. With each piece of

clothing he put on, he stamped his foot four times and
sang, "Do I look handsome? Yes, I look handsome."

When he finished, Coyote was very well dressed
indeed. That evening he went down by the spring and
waited for White Corn Girl. When she arrived with her
water jar, Coyote called out from the shadows, "White
Corn Girl, I have come to take you to my house to
marry me."

Because Coyote was so well dressed and the light
was so dim, White Corn Girl mistook him for Rainbow
Boy, but she asked, "Why have you come this evening?
You said four days, and this is only the third."

"I changed my mind," Coyote told her. "Leave your water jar and come away with me."

So White Corn Girl went away with Coyote. He took her to his house. It was dark and musty inside Coyote's house. Instead of bright birds on the rungs of the ladder, there were dead chickens. The bones of mice and prairie dogs were scattered all over the floor.

White Corn Girl began to cry. Coyote offered her dry rabbit feet and bird wings. "Don't cry," he told her. "See what fine gifts I have for you."

But White Corn Girl sobbed, "Take me back. You are not Rainbow Boy. This isn't the house I want to live in."

Coyote was afraid Rainbow Boy would hear her cries and come to punish him, so he led White Corn Girl back to the spring.

The next evening Rainbow Boy came for White Corn Girl, just as he had promised. They went to his home in the sky and they are living there still.

And now, whenever the people of the pueblo dance for rain, White Corn Girl hears the sound of their drums and their voices singing. She asks Rainbow Boy to send his cousins the clouds to freshen the fields of her people. Always, before the day's dancing is finished, a friendly rain will fall. And often, as the sun dips low into the west, Rainbow Boy paints one of his many-colored arcs across the sky as a greeting to the people, and a message that all is well with him and White Corn Girl.

# OLD MAN FINDS ECHO BOY

OLD MAN AND OLD WOMAN had been married for many years. The years had been good, and Old Man and Old Woman felt happy about their life. But one thing made them a little sad. They had no children. And many times they wished they had a child to add some joy to their home.

Every day Old Man would go to gather firewood near Sacred Mountain. They used some of the wood to heat the oven in which Old Woman baked bread. Some of it they used to heat the house in winter. And some of it Old Man traded to other people in the pueblo for clothes — a new blanket or a pair of moccassins or a shawl for Old Woman.

One day when Old Man arrived at his favorite wood gathering spot by Sacred Mountain he thought he heard the sound of a drum coming from far off — boom, boom, boom. "Who can be playing a drum way out here by the mountain?" he wondered. But Old Man had come to gather firewood, so he paid no more attention to the drum and set to work. Soon he had gathered a big bundle of dry sticks, so he returned home.

But the next day when he arrived at his wood gathering place, he heard the sound of drumming again — boom, boom, boom. And this time it seemed to be closer. Old Man stood and listened for a while. Then he went to work and gathered his firewood. He left without thinking any more about the drumming.

When Old Man arrived at his wood gathering place on the third day, the drumming seemed very close indeed. But he couldn't tell the direction it came from because it seemed to be sounding all around him — Boom! Boom! Boom!

And on the fourth day when Old Man went to his wood gathering place, the drumming came from right in front of him — BOOM! BOOM! BOOM!

He noticed a round hole in the ground, and when he approached the hole, he saw that there was a boy in it. The boy was dressed in beautiful clothes of white buckskin, with a bright blanket wrapped around his shoulders and a parrot feather in his hair. The boy was playing a drum and dancing to its rhythm. He looked up at Old Man and smiled.

Old Man was amazed. "What a fine looking boy!" he said.

The boy kept drumming and dancing, and he said exactly what Old Man had said, "What a fine looking boy!"

Old Man was surprised by that, but he knew that small children will sometimes say surprising things. He looked kindly at the boy and asked, "Where do you come from?"

The boy drummed and danced and said, "Where do you come from?"

Old Man smiled. "I think I'll take you home with me," he said.

"I think I'll take you home with me," repeated the boy.

Old Man wrapped the boy in his blanket and slinging him over his shoulder started for home. Inside the blanket the boy kept drumming — BOOM! BOOM! BOOM! And Old Man could feel the boy's legs dancing up and down as he walked along.

When Old Man got home, Old Woman came out to meet him. "Why didn't you bring any firewood?" she asked.

"Why didn't you bring any firewood?" said a voice from inside the blanket.

Old Man unwrapped the blanket. "I found this boy out by Sacred Mountain," he told Old Woman.

The boy danced and drummed and said, "I found this boy out by Sacred Mountain."

Old Woman looked at the boy, and then back at her husband. "He says everything we say."

"He says everything we say."

"Yes," said Old Man, "let's call him Echo Boy."

And the boy said, "Yes, let's call him Echo Boy."

So Old Man and Old Woman took Echo Boy inside and washed him and fed him. All day long they sat admiring him like their own child. When evening came, Old Woman took Echo Boy into another room and showed him a soft bed laid out on the floor. She told him, "This is where you will sleep."

"This is where you will sleep," said Echo Boy.

But Echo Boy didn't sleep. All night long he danced and played his drum — BOOM! BOOM! BOOM! And in the next room, Old Man and Old Woman didn't sleep either. The next morning Old Man looked at Old Woman with tired eyes and said, "This Echo Boy is very strange. I'd better tell the Elders of the pueblo about him."

So Old Man went and told the leading men of the pueblo about the boy he had found out by Sacred

Mountain. The Elders told Old Man to bring Echo Boy to meet them in the Kiva. When Old Man arrived at the Kiva with Echo Boy, all the leaders had gathered there. They all sat around the edge of the room, and Echo Boy stood in the center, dancing and drumming.

One of the Elders said, "Maybe our enemies have sent this boy."

Echo Boy said as he danced and drummed, "Maybe our enemies have sent this boy."

Another Elder said, "I think this boy is a witch."

"I think this boy is a witch."

"This boy is crazy!" said another.

"This boy is crazy!" said Echo Boy.

Then the wisest of all the Elders said, "This is a spirit boy. He should be returned to Sacred Mountain."

Echo Boy didn't dance. He didn't drum. He said nothing. And everyone knew that the wisest of the Elders had spoken the truth.

Old Man wrapped Echo Boy back up in his blanket and returned with him to Sacred Mountain. All the way, Echo Boy lay quietly in the blanket. He didn't speak until Old Man unwrapped the blanket and placed him back in the round hole in the ground. Then Echo Boy told Old Man that whenever anyone from the pueblo was in great need of clothing — a shirt or moccassins or a warm blanket or whatever — they should come to that spot and call out what they needed. Echo Boy would give it to them.

So from that day on if someone needed clothes and was too poor to buy them, they would go out by

Sacred Mountain and call, "I need a blanket," or "I
need a shirt."

From far away a voice would call back, "I need
a blanket . . . I need a shirt . . ." And in four days the
clothes that had been asked for would be waiting for
the needy person.

But this all happened a long, long time ago and
there is probably no one living today who remembers
how to find Echo Boy's special spot near the bottom of
Sacred Mountain.

# TURKEY GIRL GOES TO THE DANCES

ONCE THERE WAS A YOUNG GIRL living across the fields from the pueblo, in a small hut made of sticks. Everyone called her Turkey Girl.

Turkey Girl had no family to take care of her. The only way she was able to live was by tending turkey flocks for the people, for in those times the birds we call wild turkeys lived as tame animals in the pueblos.

In return for her work, the people gave Turkey Girl old, worn out clothes and scraps of food. But no

one treated Turkey Girl as a friend, and they certainly didn't invite her to join in any of the dances or gatherings in the pueblo.

Turkey Girl's only friends were the big birds she took care of every day. She often talked to the turkeys and told them how lonely and unhappy she was. The turkeys would cock their heads to one side and gobble softly as if they could understand what she said.

One day messengers from a neighboring pueblo came with news that in four days they were going to hold dances. Everyone from Turkey Girl's pueblo was invited. Turkey Girl heard the news and wished she could go to the dances, but she knew she would just look foolish in her ragged clothes. And besides, everyone would expect Turkey Girl to stay and mind the turkeys while they were at the dances. Turkey Girl was very sad.

And she was even sadder four days later when she saw all the people leaving the pueblo for the dances, dressed in the their prettiest clothes. Turkey Girl sat down on a rock and held her face in her hands and began to cry.

Just then the biggest turkey in the flock ran up to Turkey Girl and started pecking at her head. And then another one did too. Turkey Girl thought, "Even the turkeys are turning against me. Well, let them. I don't care if they kill me." She didn't try to run away.

But the turkeys weren't trying to hurt Turkey Girl. They were pulling the knots out of her hair, and combing it smooth with their beaks. After they combed

Turkey Girl's hair out straight, the turkeys all turned and ran toward the river.

Turkey Girl followed them, and when she reached the riverbank, the turkeys all rushed up to her and pushed her into the water. They wouldn't let her come back out onto the shore until she was washed clean by the river.

Just when Turkey Girl stepped out onto the bank of the river, the biggest turkey gobbled loudly and flapped his wings. A pair of high white buckskin moccasins fell from under his wings. They were the finest moccasins Turkey Girl had ever seen. A second turkey gobbled, and when he flapped his wings a tightly woven white manta fell to the ground. Another turkey dropped a dance sash, and another turquoise and shell beads. Soon a beautiful dance costume lay on the ground in front of Turkey Girl.

Turkey Girl dressed herself in the beautiful clothes. She thanked the turkeys over and over, and then hurried off to the dances.

At the dances, everywhere Turkey Girl walked a group of young men followed her. Everyone wondered who she was, and every young man hoped to get a chance to talk to her. Soon the boys began pushing and shoving one another, trying to get close to Turkey Girl. Finally an argument started between two young men, and then they began to fight.

Turkey Girl was frightened. She ran away from the dances and back to the turkey flock. She sat on the same rock where she had begun the day crying,

and the turkeys gathered around her. She told them breathlessly about all that had happened at the dances.

Just then some people who had left the dances early came by. They recognized Turkey Girl. They said among themselves, "Turkey Girl is a witch. See how she turned herself into a beautiful girl to go to the dances and cause trouble among the young men!"

They hurried back to tell everyone what they had discovered. When the people heard the news, they all set out to catch Turkey Girl and punish her for being a witch.

But the turkeys knew what was happening, and they led Turkey Girl away toward the mountains. When the people arrived at the turkey pens, they saw Turkey Girl and her flock far away. The people tried to follow, but couldn't overtake them.

And Turkey Girl was never seen again. No one knew what became of her. Maybe she spent the rest of her life in the mountains with her only true friends, the turkeys. Maybe she is living there still.

But they do know that the turkeys never returned to live in the pueblos. And now, if someone wants to eat turkey, or wants feathers for a blanket, or a turkey wing bone to make a flute with, they have to go turkey hunting in the mountains. And wild turkeys are not easy to catch.

# THE
# PRAIRIE DOGS
# CHASE THE
# CLOUDS AWAY

ONCE MANY PRAIRIE DOGS had a village in a wide valley to the west of a range of high mountains. One day when the prairie dogs came up out of their holes to greet the morning, they saw clouds in the sky above them. The prairie dogs were happy. They knew the clouds would bring some rain. The rain would make the grass grow. The grass would give them seeds to eat, and they would all be fat, with round bellies.

Sure enough, it began to rain. It rained all day long and all through the night. The next morning when the prairie dogs came up out of their holes, they were not so happy. There were puddles all around, and they got their feet wet before they could get down their holes again.

On the third morning, when the prairie dogs came out and saw that it was still raining, they were very unhappy. They were covered with mud before they could get back down their holes.

And when the prairie dogs came outside on the fourth morning and it was still raining, they knew they had to do something to stop the rain. If they didn't, their holes would fill up with water and they would have no place to live.

So the prairie dogs all got together in a big room underground to talk about how they could stop the rain. But no one knew how to make rain stop. Then one prairie dog said that he would go and talk to the burrowing owl. The burrowing owl is just a little bird that lives in a hole like a prairie dog, but he is an owl and he is wise. He would know what they should do.

The prairie dog ran off and found the little owl and told him all about their troubles. The owl turned his head from one side to the other as he listened. Then he said he knew exactly what they should do.

The burrowing owl came to the prairie dog village. The first thing he told them to do was go around and catch a lot of bugs. But they couldn't be just any old bugs. They had to be the shiny black bugs that go

walking along the ground in summer. If you bother those bugs, they stop and stick their tails up in the air. If you touch their tails with your fingers, your fingers will smell terrible! They are stink bugs!

The prairie dogs ran around and caught a big pile of stink bugs. The owl said that each prairie dog should fill a little sack with stink bugs and stand in front of his hole holding the sack. The owl would flap his wings one time, and they should all shake their sacks. He would flap his wings again, and they should hit their sacks with a stick. He would flap his wings one more time and they should open their sacks. But they had better hold their noses. It would smell terrible!

So every prairie dog filled a sack with stink bugs. They all stood in front of their holes holding the sacks. The owl flapped his wings one time, and they shook the sacks. He flapped his wings again, and they hit the sacks with a stick. He flapped his wings again! They opened the sacks and held their noses. It smelled terrible!

The smell rose into the sky. The dark clouds turned a little pale when they smelled that! The owl said it looked like the trick was working, and they should try again.

So the prairie dogs closed up their sacks and held the sacks in front of them. The owl flapped his wings, and they shook. He flapped again, and they hit the sacks. He flapped his wings again! They opened their sacks and held their noses. It smelled terrible!

The smell rose into the sky, and the clouds began to move away from the prairie dog village. The prairie dogs all cheered! But the owl told them they had better not stop. He said they had better try it again.

The prairie dogs closed their sacks again. The owl flapped his wings . . . once . . . twice . . . three times. They opened their sacks and held their noses. It smelled terrible!

The smell rose into the sky, and the clouds moved way back by the mountains. But the owl reminded them that if you really want something to work, you have to do it four times!

Once again they closed the sacks. They held the sacks in front of them. The owl flapped his wings, and they shook the sacks. He flapped his wings again, and they hit the sacks with a stick. The owl flapped his wings again! They opened the sacks and held their noses. It smelled TERRIBLE!

The smell rose into the sky, and the clouds disappeared behind the mountains.

And ever since that day the clouds have remembered that even though rain is a good thing, too much of anything is not good. And the clouds don't stay around too long. But there are times when the clouds forget. They stay around longer than we want them to, and we have to tell this story to remind them. Then they go away.

# THE
# BUTTERFLIES
# TRICK COYOTE

LONG AGO HUNDREDS AND HUNDREDS of butterflies lived in the valley of the Salt Lake. At one end of that valley there is a shallow lake of very salty water, and the ground around the edge of the lake is covered with white crystals of salt. In the old days people came to the lake from many miles away to gather salt for cooking. Sooner or later everybody had to visit the valley of the Salt Lake because everyone who wants to cook good food needs to have salt — even Coyote.

At that time Coyote and his wife were living just across the hill from a pueblo. One morning when Coyote was sleeping in the sun in front of his house, men with loud voices went through the pueblo calling out that in four days there would be dances. Coyote's wife heard the announcement, and she knew that the women of the pueblo would be spending the next four days baking bread and cooking delicious food for the dances. She wanted to cook some good food too, but there wasn't any salt in the house.

So Coyote's wife woke up her husband and told him, "The people in the pueblo are going to dance soon, and I want to have some good food ready. Take your sack and travel south to the Salt Lake and bring me some salt. But don't take a long time to make the trip. The dances will begin in four days."

Coyote yawned and stretched and then picked up a sack and ran off to the south. Now, Coyote can't do many things well, but one thing he can do is run. The sun was still high in the sky when he arrived at the Salt Lake, huffing and puffing.

Coyote said to himself, "I'm too tired! I'll rest here at the edge of the lake for a while. Then I'll fill my sack and run home." Coyote lay down to rest, and soon fell asleep.

The butterflies who lived in the valley saw Coyote asleep by the edge of the lake and they all came and flew around him. "Look at that lazy Coyote," they all said, "sleeping in the middle of the day. He doesn't deserve any salt."

Then the butterflies decided to play a trick on Coyote. They flew down and landed on Coyote, until he was covered with bright little butterflies. Each butterfly took hold of one of Coyote's hairs. Then the butterflies all flew up into the air, carrying Coyote with them.

They flew back to Coyote's house near the pueblo. Then they flew down and left Coyote on the very spot where he had been sleeping earlier that day. The butterflies flew back to the valley of the Salt Lake laughing so hard they couldn't fly in a straight line.

When the sun went down the cool air woke Coyote up. He looked all about him scratching his head. "How did I get here?" he wondered. Then he shrugged. "Maybe I just dreamed that my wife needed salt and I ran all the way to the Salt Lake."

But when his wife came around the corner of the house, he knew it hadn't been a dream. She began to shake him and scold, "You lazy old man! Why didn't you go to the Salt Lake?"

Coyote was very puzzled. But since it was too late to go back to the lake that day, he just promised his wife he'd leave early the next morning and be sure to bring her a big sack of salt.

The next morning Coyote's wife made sure he was up early and on his way to the Salt Lake. Coyote ran even faster this time and arrived at the lake so tired he could hardly stand up. But he set to work filling his sack.

After he had put a few handfuls of salt into the sack, Coyote sighed, "I'm too tired! I'll have to rest before I finish filling my sack."

Again Coyote fell asleep beside the lake, and the butterflies saw him. "Let's trick that Coyote again," they said.

They all flew down and landed on Coyote. They flew up and away, carrying Coyote back to his house. They set him down on the roof of his house, right next to the ladder that led inside. Then the butterflies returned to the valley of the Salt Lake, zigzagging and darting all about because they were laughing so hard.

Later that day Coyote's wife came back from the spring with her water jar and found him asleep on the roof. She was so angry she dumped her water all over him. "You lazy old man! Next time I'll break my water jar over your head! Go get me some salt!"

Coyote wrinkled his brow and shook his head. "I'm sure I ran to the Salt Lake today," he said. "My legs are aching and my lungs burn." But soon he went back to sleep thinking, "Tomorrow I'll get my wife a big sack of salt."

The next day when Coyote arrived at the Salt Lake he was so tired he couldn't even see. But he scratched and pawed and filled his sack with salt. He turned to go home.

But after he'd taken a couple steps, Coyote moaned, "I'm too tired! I could never make it home without some rest." He dropped his sack and fell to the ground exhausted and was soon asleep.

The butterflies flew down and landed all over him. They rose into the air and away they flew to Coyote's house. They carried him down through the door in the roof and into the house. They swooped and fluttered as they flew back to the valley of the Salt Lake.

Luckily Coyote woke up before his wife found him asleep. He had no idea what had happened, but he knew he'd better not let his wife catch him without any salt. So Coyote climbed the ladder and started right back to the Salt Lake. He got there at nightfall, and there was his sack of salt lying beside the lake.

Coyote was so tired he stumbled over the sack and fell down. Before he even hit the ground, he was sound asleep.

This time the butterflies felt sorry for Coyote. They flew down and landed all over him. And they landed all over his sack of salt too. They flew up and away to Coyote's house. They left him and his sack of salt beside the door.

When he woke up and saw where he was, Coyote groaned, "Oh, no! How can this be? I'm positive I went to the Salt Lake." Then he saw the sack of salt beside him. "Well," he shrugged, "I must have run all the way home without remembering it."

Coyote gave the sack of salt to his wife, and she went to work cooking and baking. All through the next day she worked, and on the following day when they heard the sound of drums coming from the pueblo, Coyote and his wife danced round and round their house. Every time they stopped to rest, they ate some of the food Coyote's wife had cooked.

And in the valley of the Salt Lake, the butterflies are still laughing so hard about the good trick they played on Coyote that they can never go in a straight line. All day long they swoop and zigzag and they dart this way and that as they fly.

# NOTES ON THE STORIES

## THE SINGING WAGON

This story comes from Elsie Clews Parsons' *Tewa Tales*.
My main addition to the story is the series of animals that come
to help push the wagon. In the original only Coyote helps. Also,
the original ends with Black Beetle Old Man and Black Beetle
Old Woman falling asleep while singing to the doll and then
being killed by a passerby during the night. *(Adapted with permission of the American Folk-Lore Society.)*

## BE CAREFUL WITH PROMISES

This simple teaching tale has been collected at several
pueblos. There is a version in Ahlee James' *Tewa Firelight Tales*
and two in Ruth Benedict's *Tales of the Cochiti Indians*. I expanded the song so that listeners could participate.

## CLAY OLD MAN AND CLAY OLD WOMAN

This is the only tale in this collection that belongs to the
body of creation and migration stories. Often a different set of
rules govern the time when such stories can be told. In *Finding
the Center*, Dennis Tedlock reports that at Zuni such "in the
beginning stories" can be told year round, while most other tales
are restricted to winter evenings. A man from San Juan Pueblo
has told me just the opposite is true of his Pueblo. This story is
based on a tale and information gleaned from the notes in Ruth
Benedict's *Tales of the Cochiti Indians*.

## FROG AND LOCUST

This story appears in other collections of Pueblo tales. The source for all appears to be Hattie G. Lockett's "The Unwritten Literature of the Hopis," although I made the story more repetitive. The theme of cooperation expressed in this story is an important one to the Pueblo Indians, who were village dwelling farmers.

## CLAY POT BOY

The theme of a girl who has no interest in boys and ends up bearing a child to a supernatural father is a common one in stories of Pueblo and other Southwestern Indian groups. Often the father is the Sun or the Rain. "Clay Pot Boy" is adapted from "Water Jar Boy" in Elsie Clews Parsons' *Tewa Tales*. She collected it from western Tewas living at Hano, a Tewa enclave among the Hopi. *(Adapted with permission of the American Folk-Lore Society.)*

## A HEART FULL OF TURQUOISE

Every pueblo has a story of a giant who wants to carry children off. They use it to frighten the children into behaving, and if the story alone isn't effective, a man will put on the giant's costume and mask and make an appearance at the house of the uncooperative child. The image of an evil person's heart being filled with thorns, and the replacing of thorns with turquoise, occurs frequently in Pueblo stories. This story is mainly derived from Ruth Benedict's *Tales of the Cochiti Indians*.

## THE GIRL WHO MARRIED THE RAINBOW

This story belongs to the group of wife stealer stories which are very common throughout the pueblos. Often the one who steals the wife is supernatural and the husband has to perform great feats (frequently with the help of Spider Woman) to get her back. This telling most closely resembles "Light of the Evening and Rainbow" in Elizabeth Willis DeHuff's *Tay-Tay's Memories*.

71

## OLD MAN FINDS ECHO BOY

This story is adapted from one in Elsie Clews Parsons' *Taos Tales*. As with most of the stories, I have added incidents to make the story feel more complete. I added a more conclusive ending as well. *(Adapted with permission of the American Folk-Lore Society.)*

## TURKEY GIRL GOES TO THE DANCES

The tale of Turkey Girl is very widespread among the pueblos, and I have heard one Navajo version as well. It is often identified as a story of European origin brought into the Southwest by the Spanish. The Cinderella parallels are obvious, and in some versions, such as Ahlee James' in *Tewa Firelight Tales*, the similarity to the Old World story is very great. The best known version of this tale is in Frank Cushing's *Zuni Folk Tales*. My telling mixes elements from several sources.

## THE PRAIRIE DOGS CHASE THE CLOUDS AWAY

This story is based loosely on "The Prairie Dogs and their Priest, the Burrowing Owl" in Frank Cushing's *Zuni Folk Tales*. The general plot of the prairie dogs being threatened by too much rain and the burrowing owl using "stink bugs" to drive the clouds away are from the source. I have added the repetitive pattern of the story, however. I have been told by a woman from Acoma that they also tell a story in which "stink bugs" save the world from a flood.

## THE BUTTERFLIES TRICK COYOTE

This story follows the common pattern of some weak little animals making a fool of Coyote. It also reveals Coyote's neglect of proper ritual conduct. He should have approached the Salt Lake reverently and left an offering by the lake to thank Salt Woman for sharing her gift of salt. And, of course, sleeping during the daytime would only be permissible if one were very sick. The source of this story is Elsie Clews Parsons' *Tewa Tales*. *(Adapted with permission of the American Folk-Lore Society.)*

# BIBLIOGRAPHY

BENEDICT, RUTH. *Tales of the Cochiti Indians.* Smithsonian Institution Bureau of American Ethnology Bulletin 98, 1931.

CUSHING, FRANK HAMILTON. *Zuni Folk Tales.* New York: G.P. Putnam & Sons, 1901.

DE HUFF, ELIZABETH WILLIS. *Taytay's Memories.* New York: Harcourt Brace & Co., 1924.

JAMES, AHLEE. *Tewa Firelight Tales.* New York: Longmans, 1927.

PARSONS, ELSIE CLEWS. *Tewa Tales.* Memoirs, 19. New York: American Folk-Lore Society, 1926.

_____. *Taos Tales.* Memoirs 34. New York: American Folk-Lore Society, 1940.

TEDLOCK, DENNIS. *Finding the Center: Narrative Poetry of the Zuni Indians.* New York: Dial, 1972.

# THE ILLUSTRATOR

Lucy Jelinek is an artist-designer who has worked in New Mexico since 1978. Her company, Santa Fe Pre-Print, is a graphic design firm specializing in publications. *A Heart Full Of Turquoise* is the eighth book she has designed and illustrated for Joe Hayes.

# THE PUBLISHER

Mariposa Printing & Publishing was established in 1980. Our goal is to provide quality commercial printing to the Santa Fe community and to provide quality-crafted, limited edition publications in various literary fields.

Your comments and suggestions are appreciated. Contact Joe Mowrey, owner-production manager, Mariposa Printing & Publishing, 922 Baca Street, Santa Fe, New Mexico, (505) 988-5582.